CONTENTS

FOREWORD

When President Barack Obama stated in November 2010 that "India is not emerging; India has emerged," he echoed an idea espoused by an array of American personalities, from Thomas Friedman to Warren Buffett. Around the world, interest in India's economy has been growing, and rightly so: according to a 2011 report by Citigroup, India may be on a path to surpass China as the world's largest economy by 2050.

But for all the public attention surrounding India's growth rate in recent years, misconceptions remain about what propels it. In the West, many perceive the Indian economy's dynamism as driven by the information technology (IT) sector, when in fact that industry accounted for only 7.5 percent of India's GDP and employs a meager 3 million people. While Indian IT was the first industry to take off after the liberalization of the economy in the early 1990s, some 20 years later, the singular emphasis on IT has become outdated.

Another prevalent misconception in the West is to regard India as a cheap labor-driven economy that outsources jobs from other countries. In the aftermath of President Obama's 2010 trip to India and the conclusion of several business deals worth $10 billion between the two countries, nearly 54,000 jobs were created in the United States. Furthermore, according to a report by the Confederation of Indian Industry (CII), since 2005 nearly two-thirds of Indian companies have added jobs to their U.S. operations. Together, these companies employ more than 60,000 people across 40 U.S. states and have saved some 2,600 jobs from being eliminated due to their acquisition of U.S. firms.

In reality, many facets of the emerging Indian economy remain relatively unexamined, rendering explanations of the country's complicated growth story incomplete. Having attracted more than $1 billion worth of U.S. foreign direct investment (FDI) in the short period from April to December 2010, the Indian economy increasingly carries the interests of hundreds of major U.S. companies in many sectors. The growing investment of the United States and the rest of the world in the Indian market lend impetus to an examination of India's economy beyond IT.

The Wadhwani Chair in U.S.-India Policy at CSIS therefore embarked on a signature lecture series to provide an in-depth perspective on India's economic future by examining developments in underexplored sectors of the Indian economy. The program, directed by Wadhwani Chair Fellow Persis Khambatta, brought together industry leaders, policymakers, and public citizens via this high-profile speaker series, both in Washington, D.C., and New Delhi, to address the complexities as well as highlight the challenges and areas of untapped potential in India's burgeoning economy.

Listed below are the sectors of the Indian economy chosen for the first tranche of the signature lecture series, along with their accomplished and able speakers. After an introduction by Persis Khambatta that highlights their key thoughts and recommendations, the full text of their remarks follows.

India's Energy Options: New Sources, Innovations, and Areas of Cooperation
Vikram Mehta, chairman, Shell Group of Companies, India

India on the Move: Infrastructure for the 21st Century
Rajiv Lall, managing director and CEO, Infrastructure Development Finance Company, Ltd., India

India on the Move: Infrastructure for the 21st Century (Part II)
John Flannery, president and CEO, General Electric India

The United States and India: Innovating Health Care
Pratap C. Reddy, chairman, Apollo Hospitals Group, India

The United States, India, and the Future of Automotive Manufacturing
Arvind Goel, president and head business group, Tata AutoComp Systems, Ltd.

Taken together, these five lectures provide invaluable insights into key sectors of India's emerging economy. These sectors will, if fully developed, not only dramatically improve the lives of the Indian people, but also help India fully realize its potential to be a true economic powerhouse in the 21st century.

Karl F. Inderfurth
Wadhwani Chair in U.S.-India Policy Studies, CSIS

ACKNOWLEDGMENTS

In preparing this report, I received invaluable assistance from many colleagues and friends in both Washington, D.C., and India who deserve recognition. First and foremost, I would like to thank Ambassador Karl F. Inderfurth for his wholehearted support, insight, and guidance throughout the series. I would also like to thank the GE Foundation for their generous support of the Emerging Indian Economy Signature Speaker Series, and for enabling CSIS to host senior executives in both countries. I am also grateful for the support of the Confederation of Indian Industry, especially Chandrajit Banerjee, Sandhya Satwadi, Aditya Vemulapalli, and Sumani Dash.

Each speaker engaged in extensive question-and-answer sessions in order to get the most out of each interaction. In order of presentation, the speakers included: Vikram Singh Mehta, former chairman of the Shell Group of Companies, India; Rajiv Lall, managing director and CEO of Infrastructure Development Finance Company, Ltd., India; John Flannery, president and CEO of GE India; Pratap C. Reddy, chairman of the Apollo Hospitals Group, India; and Arvind Goel, president and head Business Group of TATA AutoComp Systems Ltd. I am grateful to each of them for their participation, their willingness to answer difficult questions, and their ability to condense large amounts of unwieldy information into a concise, clear set of remarks.

The majority of this report results from a series of on-the-record public events, for which the speakers prepared remarks. However, some of the information here results from informal, not-for-attribution discussions in both Washington and New Delhi, including experts in both the government and private sector. Genuine thanks to everyone who gave generously of their time to participate in these sessions. In particular, I would like to thank Ambassador H. K. Singh and Aman Raj Khanna at the Indian Council for Research and International Economic Relations (ICRIER) for their support and hospitality in hosting part of the series in New Delhi.

This report was a team effort, and all the staff of the Wadhwani Chair in U.S.-India Studies contributed to it. Particular thanks to Nick Lombardo for providing exceptional support throughout the process; and Sameer Punyani, whose contributions as a researcher, analyst, writer, and editor were invaluable. Niraj Patel, Justin Painter, Jesse Sedler, and Ritika Bhasker also provided helpful support during their internships. The CSIS Strategic Planning team was instrumental in preparing this report; I would like to especially thank Johanna Nesseth and Eric Palomaa for their support and guidance throughout. Lastly, I would like to thank the Wadhwani Foundation for their support of this project and their dedication to advancing the U.S.-India relationship.

Persis Khambatta
Fellow
Wadhwani Chair in U.S.-India Policy Studies, CSIS

INTRODUCTION

As a large emerging economy with a growing middle class, India has captured the attention of developed economies eager to tap into a new market with hundreds of millions of potential consumers. Within Asia, policymakers and private companies alike look to India as a regional market for exports and large-scale projects. India has also increasingly emphasized strategic economic relations in the region, most notably with Afghanistan, Pakistan, China, and the Association of Southeast Asian Nations (ASEAN).

The excitement India's economy has generated lately is due in large part to changing internal and external dynamics. By some estimates, India's economy will grow from its current $1.8 trillion GDP to be the world's third largest in 2030, with a GDP of close to $30 trillion.[1] Correspondingly, North America and Western Europe's share of global GDP is expected to shrink from 41 percent to 18 percent, while "developing Asia" will grow from 27 percent to 49 percent.[2] India's exports of goods and services have risen from 8 percent of GDP to 25 percent in the last two decades alone.[3] In addition, its exports are more diversified—both geographically and in terms of the products it sells—than its neighbors and competitors.[4] Many believe India could be the rising economic powerhouse that China is seen as today.[5] There is broad agreement that the global center of economic activity and growth is moving to Asia, and investors are increasingly looking to India for economic and trade opportunities.

Internally, India's prospects remain bright as the middle class continues to expand and the benefits of their participation in the economy spread throughout the country—a more highly educated middle class has encouraged growth in dynamic sectors of the economy and boosted entrepreneurship and consumption. India's young population constitutes two-thirds of the total populace; the nearly 800 million Indians under 35 will be an important engine of the country's economic future. Often referred to as a "demographic dividend," this massive young set could translate into an equally massive workforce in the coming decades.

---

1. Standard Chartered Bank, "The Super-Cycle Report," November 15, 2010, 5, http://www.standard-chartered.com/id/_documents/press-releases/en/The%20Super-cycle%20Report-12112010-final.pdf. By other estimates, India's economy is projected to grow from its current GDP of $4 trillion (in PPP terms) to nearly $86 trillion by 2050, edging out China to become the world's largest economy.

2. Knight Frank and Citi Private Bank, "Wealth Report 2012," 12, http://www.thewealthreport.net/. Measured in purchasing power parity (PPP) terms.

3. World Bank Data Catalog, "Exports of Goods and Services (% of GDP)," http://data.worldbank.org/indicator/NE.EXP.GNFS.ZS/countries/1W-IN?page=4&display=default.

4. Anoop Singh, "India: Linked or De-linked from the Global Economy," IMF Direct, October 25, 2012, http://blog-imfdirect.imf.org/2011/10/25/india-linked-or-de-linked-from-the-global-economy/.

5. National Intelligence Council, *Global Trends 2030: Alternative Worlds* (Washington, D.C.: Office of the Director of National Intelligence, December 2012), 16, http://www.dni.gov/files/documents/GlobalTrends_2030.pdf.

Figure 1: BRICS GDP Growth

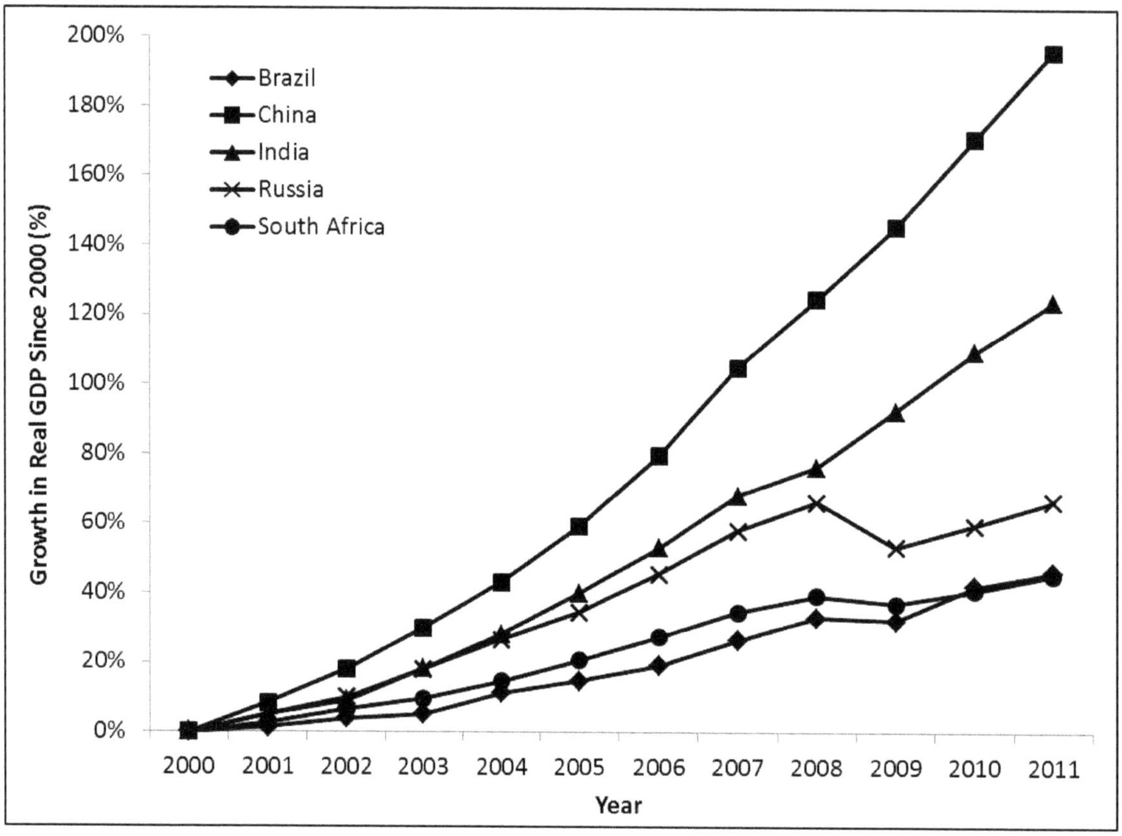

India's economy doubled in size from 2000 to 2010, outpacing all other BRICS countries except China.

Source: United Nations Conference on Trade & Development, UNCTADStat, http://unctadstat.unctad.org/ReportFolders/reportFolders.aspx, analysis by CSIS.

The rising role of India's states has also served to shift internal dynamics. Many of India's states are as large as nations, and although New Delhi controls the budget for needed reforms and oversight, the implementation strategies for many important issues are largely left to state governments. As policymakers push through economic reforms, knowing which states will execute them with a business- and development-friendly approach is integral to navigating India's complex environment.

The outlook is not all upbeat, though. The widespread hope that the United Progressive Alliance (UPA) coalition government, led by the Congress Party, would focus on reforms after their reelection in 2009 were dashed when it became clear that energy was instead being put toward building more social-welfare programs,[6] creating more pressure on the fiscal deficit and even greater dependency on an already financially strained government. However, the latter half of 2012 saw a reinvigorated push for economic reforms by Prime Minister Manmohan Singh, together

6. Hemant Krishan Singh,"India's Prevailing Political Economy: The Logic of Reform," *ICRIER Issue Brief*, vol. 1, issue 1 (October 18, 2011), http://www.icrier.org/icrier_wadhwani/Index_files/ICRIER-Wadhwani%20Chair-%20ISSUE%20BRIEF-OCT%202011.pdf.

Figure 2: BRICS Power Distribution and Transmission Losses

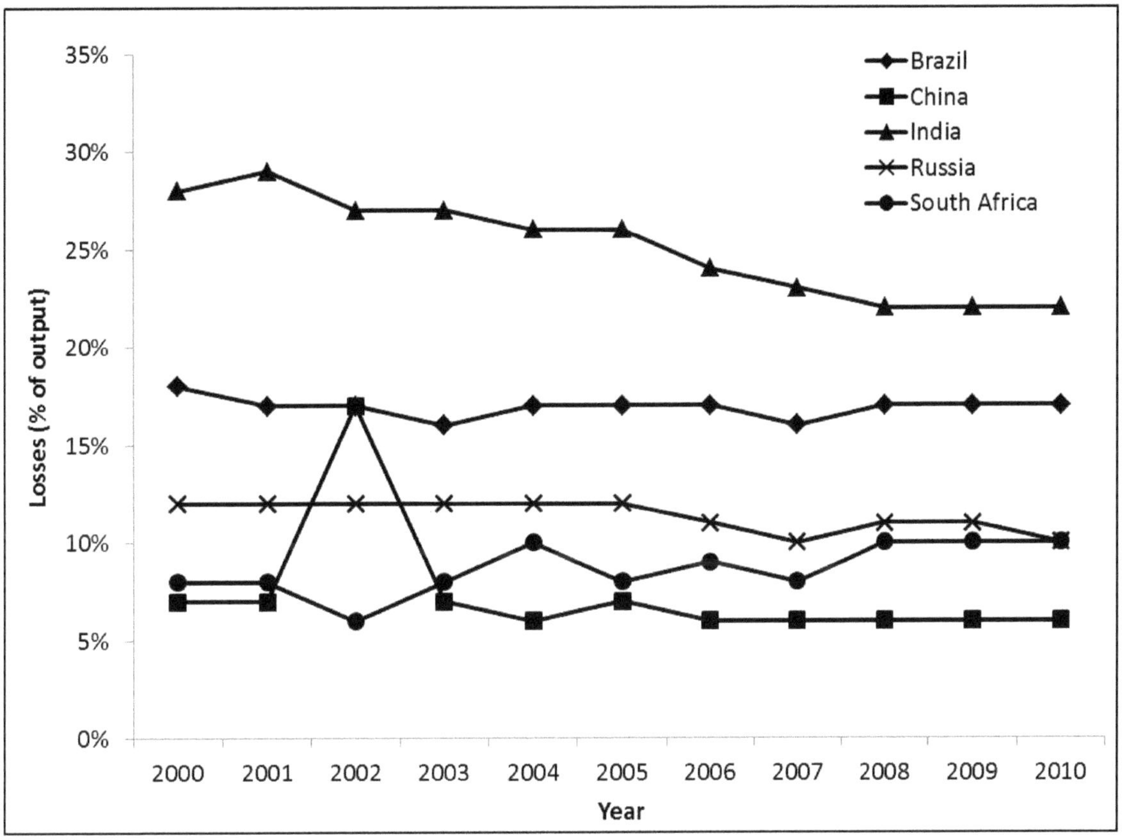

Although India has improved recently, compared to other emerging economies it still suffers from significant electric power distribution losses.

Source: The World Bank Group, Databank, http://databank.worldbank.org/ddp/home.do.

capacity is based on expensive and polluting diesel generation.[10] As the massive July 2012 blackouts illustrated, India's struggle with an unreliable power grid and insufficient capacity for power generation can have dramatic consequences.[11]

India's oil companies are aggressively pursuing overseas assets in order to increase supply, but politics and nationalist tendencies often intervene in an unhelpful manner. With insufficient domestic oil and gas reserves and blocked access to existing domestic coal supply, India will have to continue to import energy at a higher cost. This likely means increased engagement with the Middle East and Southeast Asia is necessary, as well as exploring the many opportunities for energy cooperation and trade that lie across South Asia.

Like many aspects of the economy, the energy sector is hindered by bureaucratic inertia and excessive government intervention. Mehta described India as a state that still wants to hold on to the energy sector; it has not allowed the private sector and the government to operate on a

10. Ibid.

11. Over the course of three days in July and August, more than 600 million people were without power. For more information, see Jim Yardley and Gardiner Harris, "2nd Day of Power Failure Cripples Wide Swath of India," *New York Times*, July 31, 2012, http://www.nytimes.com/2012/08/01/world/asia/power-outages-hit-600-million-in-india.html?pagewanted=all.

level playing field. Energy is a vital national subject handled out of New Delhi, but it needs support from state governments and the private sector, and finding the balance is a tricky endeavor. Significant subsidies on oil and other petroleum products distort market forces, and the various ministries that oversee the sector lack a coherent or strategic policy framework. While recent government reforms such as allowing FDI in power exchanges and reducing oil and fuel subsidies are steps in the right direction, structural issues still need to be addressed.

As a way forward, Mehta recommended boosting domestic production by establishing more public-private partnerships; leveraging natural gas as a bridge between current supplies and a future with renewable energy; rationalizing fuel prices; and leveraging existing technology to improve processes, including recovery rates. To emphasize its importance, Mehta suggested the creation of an energy "super-ministry," which would allow for a more strategic energy policy—currently as many as eight ministries oversee some aspect of the energy industry. If India were to create an institutional framework, it would allow for a more cohesive and integrated energy policy, and better address many of the hard truths.

Figure 3: India's Energy Production, Consumption, and Imports

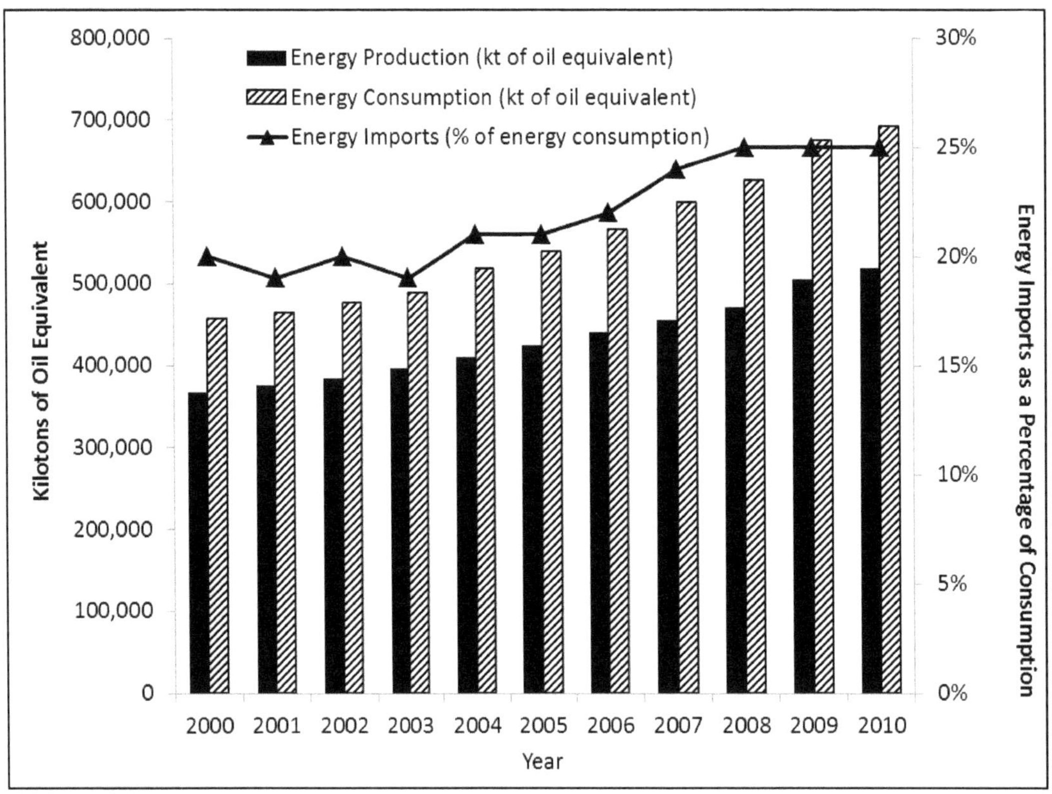

The yawning gap between energy production and consumption has required India to increase its energy imports to meet the demands of its growing economy.

Source: The World Bank Group, Databank, http://databank.worldbank.org/ddp/home.do.

India's workers will be unable to productively enter the skilled workforce. Reddy also mentioned the high cost of health care in the United States, stating that the United States does not need to spend 15 percent of its GDP on health care and that lower-cost alternatives may be an area for collaboration between the two countries' systems.

Reddy noted that India's inadequate supply of health human resources is, in fact, an area of vast opportunity. He suggested that the lack of health care workers could be made up for by enhancing the already-existing workforce under the ASHA (Accredited Social Health Activist) program, which helps implement India's National Rural Health Mission.[18] Developing India's health care human resources and using available IT innovations will play a pivotal role in not only improving health outcomes in an inclusive manner, but also ensuring robust economic growth in the health care industry and beyond.

Automotive Manufacturing

For observers of India, it is a known fact that leapfrogging is a way of life throughout the country. Many consumers who never had a land-line telephone skipped straight to mobile phones at the first chance, and young students with few scholastic resources can now leapfrog straight to the Aakash tablet. The same thing can be said of India's economic development pattern. While most societies move from agriculture to manufacturing, then to a service or knowledge-based economy as they develop, India leapfrogged from agriculture to services, and manufacturing is now expanding to fill the "missing middle." As such, the government has laid out plans to increase manufacturing's share of GDP from 16 percent to 25 percent by 2022,[19] including creating 100 million new jobs in the sector.

Arvind Goel examined both the challenges and opportunities facing India's manufacturing sector, highlighting the fact that while manufacturing's contribution to India's GDP has risen rapidly, it is still well below its potential. Manufacturing plays a crucial role in absorbing surplus labor from agriculture, and provides transitional opportunities to those seeking to join other labor-intensive sectors. Currently, agriculture employs nearly 60 percent of the Indian workforce, but contributes only 16 percent of GDP. Agriculture's contribution to GDP has stagnated at 15 percent to 16 percent since 1980, whereas others in the region have increased their share to 25 percent to 34 percent.[20] Manufacturing also has a positive multiplier effect, indirectly creating additional jobs in related activities.

As covered in previous discussions, India's power shortage weighs heavily on several other sectors, particularly manufacturing. According to Goel, power is considered a raw material for the manufacturing industry, and while some states' power-generation and distribution systems are reliable, other states grapple with a consistent power shortage of 10 percent or more. In order to address this, private industry has been impressing upon state governments the importance of reliable power for attracting industry. Many companies are forced to set up their own power plants or rely on expensive diesel generators as a workaround, increasing the cost of doing business. The

18. Ministry of Health & Family Welfare, Government of India, "About ASHA," http://www.mohfw.nic.in/NRHM/asha.htm#abt.

19. Ministry of Commerce and Industry, Government of India, "National Manufacturing Policy," November 2011, 4, http://commerce.nic.in/whatsnew/National_Manfacruring_Policy2011.pdf.

20. Ministry of Commerce and Industry, Government of India, "National Manufacturing Policy," November 2011, 1.

Figure 6: Sectoral Composition of GDP

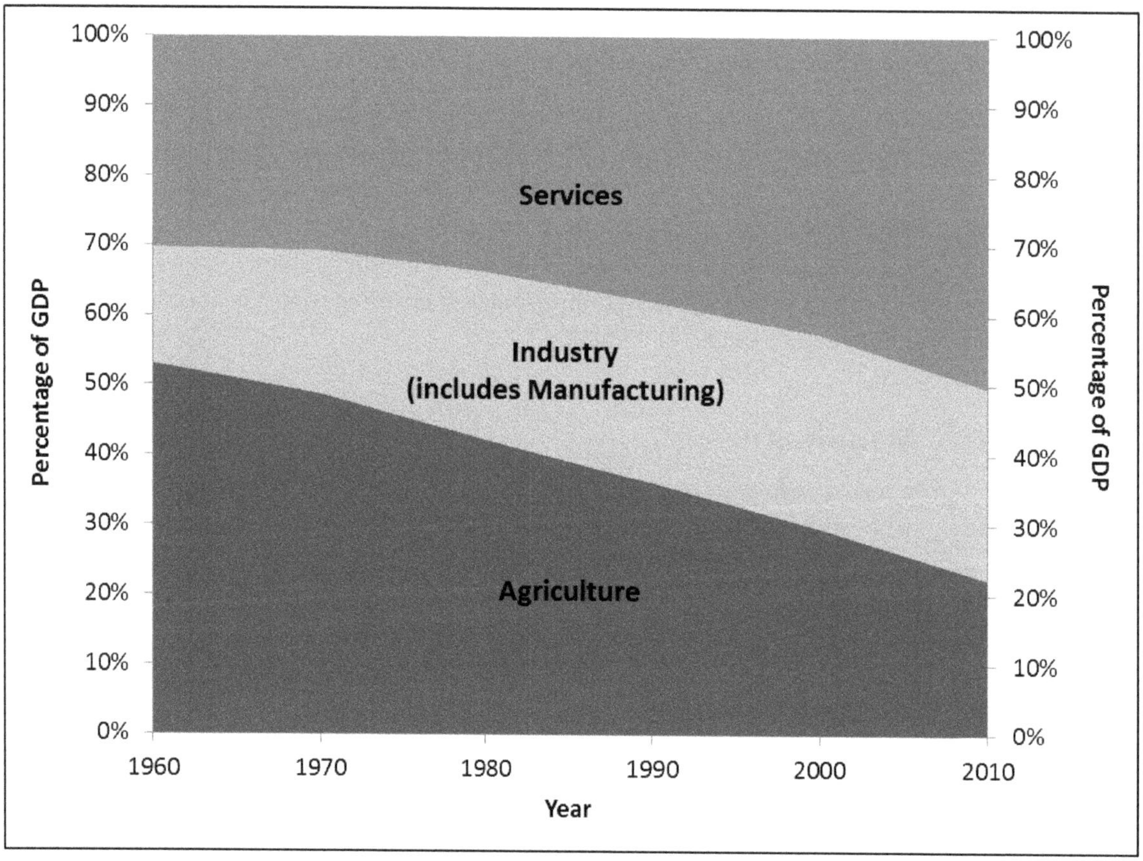

Industry and manufacturing together is slowly growing, contributing nearly 25% of GDP in 2010.

Source: India Economic Survey 2011-2012, chapter 1, table 1.6, http://indiabudget.nic.in/es2011-12/echap-01.pdf.

rising cost of power is reflected in a company's cost structure, as are considerations like the price of electronic and computerized machinery, which are used extensively and can be destroyed by frequent fluctuations in voltage.

Policy instruments are already being used under the National Manufacturing Policy. Goel highlighted the recent creation of National Investment and Manufacturing Zones (NIMZs) around the country In these special zones, state and central governments are modifying regulations on typically difficult issues such as land reform, zoning, and infrastructure to encourage greater industrial and manufacturing growth.

Goel also discussed persistently high inflation as a problem. High inflation increases capital costs for key auto-manufacturing inputs such as steel, making their already-tight margins even tighter. Stronger fiscal and monetary policy to control inflation and economic and market uncertainty would help create more stable cost structures for manufacturers.

As India's manufacturing sector continues to grow, human capital remains a major issue. Thirty-six percent of jobs in automotive manufacturing remain vacant because of a lack of skilled and 850,000 jobs every month.[23] Community colleges and vocational training institutes would be able to create synergies between industry and education, and create a more reliable pipeline of skilled workers suited to a host of different industries. "Earn and learn" schemes like the one described by Arvind Goel in his lecture, are an example of a private-sector innovation that could be expanded, with subsidies from the government, with a direct benefit to both industry and workers.

Inequality and education deficiencies are key weaknesses in India.[24] The demographics are favorable, but unless efforts to bridge the talent gap are addressed holistically and effectively, the projected "demographic dividend" could turn out to be a burden. The imagined benefits are not likely to materialize without a less onerous, centralized environment for education and skills training. In countries lacking employment opportunities, large youth populations have repeatedly caused social and political disruption, further emphasizing the need for the right kind of institutional policy framework for economic growth.

In order to meet its own goal of 10 million seats in higher education to bring India closer to the global average for Gross Enrollment Ratio,[25] India must build 1,000 universities and 50,000 colleges within the next decade.[26] It is difficult to imagine that India can do this on its own. Therefore, allowing foreign institutions to partner with Indian ones is key to meeting India's own goals. The speakers in this series, as well as higher education experts and officials, have repeatedly noted that the system is bound by too much government regulation, making it inflexible for students and industry, and unresponsive to their needs.[27]

A Final Word: Decisive Leadership Needed

There is still a long way to go in order for India to realize its potential in terms of employment, human capital, and trade. On average, 750,000 people join the job market every month, and no single industry has the capacity to absorb them all. A lack of physical and social infrastructure, good governance, bureaucratic capacity, and corruption are running themes in the lectures that follow in this report, themes that the government has emphasized in its policy pronouncements but has yet to fully operationalize effectively.

In a statement at the opening of 2012 World Economic Forum (WEF) on India, WEF Founder and Executive Chairman Klaus Schwab commented that "economic recovery is not automatically guaranteed [for India] as a cyclical process, but rather will require decisive and coordinated economic and political leadership to put the country on a different and more inclusive path for the next phase of its development."[28] India's economic growth is at an important inflection point, and how its government steers policy and reforms in the next year will affect its long-term trajectory. In the following pages, our speakers' comments and perspectives give a fuller un-

23. E-mail interview with World Bank, December 3, 2012.

24. National Intelligence Council, *Global Trends 2030,* ix.

25. Government of India Planning Commission, "Faster, Sustainable and More Inclusive Growth: An Approach to the Twelfth Five Year Plan," October, 2011, 100, http://planningcommission.nic.in/plans/planrel/12appdrft/appraoch_12plan.pdf.

26. Sabil, "Address of Mr. Kapil Sibal, Minister of HRD and C&IT at the US India Higher Education Summit."

27. Arvind Panagariya, *India: The Emerging Giant* (New York: Oxford University Press, 2008), 444–51.

28. Klaus Schwab, "India and the World Economic Forum," World Economic Forum, http://www.weforum.org/content/india-and-world-economic-forum.

derstanding of the macro- and microeconomies across India's foundational sectors, and what actions the government and the private sector should take in order to turn the potential for further economic growth into reality.

1 INDIA'S ENERGY OPTIONS: NEW SOURCES, INNOVATIONS, AND AREAS OF COOPERATION

Remarks by Vikram Mehta, chairman, Shell Group of Companies, India

October 18, 2011

Introduction

Energy sits at the nub of every policymaker's deepest dilemmas in India. How does a policymaker provide access to affordable and secure energy to the poor, without undermining the fundamentals of the market, and imposing an unacceptable burden on the exchequer? How does a policymaker accelerate economic growth without degrading the environment? How can India extract the benefits of globalization and connectivity and at the same time ensure respect and furtherance of its national self-reliance? These dilemmas are difficult to resolve. It is exceedingly difficult for a policymaker in a democratic setup to establish the balance.

These questions should be viewed through the prism of the political economy of the energy sector, by identifying the issues that India faces, by setting out the agenda that the government has laid out, and by perhaps focusing on some of the questions that will need to be resolved in the coming years—all of this within the backdrop of the Indian political economy. First, it is important to provide a profile of the energy sector.

A Profile of the Indian Energy Sector

The Indian economy has grown by 8-plus percent over the last five years. During this period, the demand for motor gasoline and diesel has gone into double digits.

The per-capita consumption of energy in India is 500 kg of oil equivalent (kgoe). The world average is 1,800 kgoe. China and the United States consume 1,090 and 7,835 kgoe, respectively.

Over the last five years, the international price of petrol, diesel, kerosene, and LPG have increased by approximately 95 percent. During this same period, the domestic prices for these four products have increased 35 to 45 percent. The difference between the international price and the domestic price has been made up through subsidies as well as losses for state-owned oil companies.

In 2009–2010, the state-owned oil companies lost $20 billion. In 2010–2011, this figure fell to $15 billion. The only reason these companies did not enter Chapter 11 was due to the IOUs and the subsidies provided by the government. The IEA has estimated that India ranks among the top-five subsidizers in the world, next only to Saudi Arabia, but above Iran.

Furthermore, the production targets for coal and oil have had to be scaled down. The Planning Commission has reduced the targets by 8 to 10 percent for both of those products. In 1980, India imported 27 percent of its crude oil requirements, today it imports 80 percent.

The IEA has estimated that the OECD countries require 1.1 barrels of oil to add $1,000 to their GDP. The equivalent is 3.3 barrels for India.

Forty-five percent of India's population is not on the commercial grid. They do not have access to commercial energy. They rely on firewood or dung to meet their fuel lighting and cooking requirements.

The contribution of hydro, nuclear, wind, solar, and biofuels comprises 7 percent of India's energy basket. The entire energy infrastructure is, in short, based on fossil fuels.

The expenditure on R&D collectively by state-owned companies over the past five years was less than $1 billion. This is less than what Shell spent on R&D in one year.

Finally, there are as many as eight different government ministries dealing with aspects of energy in India. The Ministry of Petroleum and Natural Gas, the Ministry of Coal, the Ministry of Unconventional Energy, the Ministry of Atomic Energy, the Ministry of Power, the Planning Commission, and the Prime Minister's Office. These ministries are each headed by a cabinet minister with their own bureaucracies, their own vested interests, and they each operate through their respective silos.

These facts not only provide a profile of the energy sector, but also identify five hard truths that the Indian energy sector and Indian policymakers must confront.

Five "Hard Truths" of the Indian Energy Sector

Market Demand

The first hard truth is that demand for energy is surging. The reasons for this surge are population, prosperity, and policy. The population growth rate in India has come down from 2.4 percent to 1.1 percent, but it still translated to a population of [1.2] billion people. India is entering the most energy-intensive phase of its economic development. The country has a huge plan to invest in infrastructure, manufacturing, and power plants and all of these are going to require massive amounts of energy.

But over and above that, millions of people are entering what is loosely referred to as the "middle class." These are people who have middle-class incomes—or if they don't have middle-class incomes yet, they certainly have middle-class aspirations. These are people who currently are maybe riding a bicycle, but have the aspiration to trade up to a two-wheeler and eventually to own a Nano car.

The pressure on demand for energy is going to be huge as this mass of people move from rural India to urban India, and seek to meet their aspirations. The policy environment has not been conducive to containing demand. India is amongst the largest subsidizers of petroleum products in the world. The price mechanism has not been a countervailing force. The demand has been encouraged because of the subsidies on motor fuels, on transportation fuels, and cooking fuels.

It is estimated that the demand for energy in India will grow by 400 percent between now and

2030. These estimates highlight the basic truth that India's demand position is a worry. Demand is surging, and that is something that has to be considered very carefully.

Market Supply

The second hard truth is that supplies of energy are struggling to keep pace with demand. Coal is the mainstay of India's energy-consumption basket. India has abundant coal reserves. The reserves-to-consumption ratio in coal is about 85 years; and, in principle, India should not have concerns about coal energy.

But there are three major blockers to realizing the potential of coal.

The first is that the coal mines are located hundreds of miles from the main consumption centers. They are also located in areas that are currently facing social unrest. The Maoist movement in India is concentrated in those areas where coal mines are located.

The second problem is that the infrastructure for bringing the coal from the production point, from the pit head, to the consumption center is relatively weak and inadequate. Recently it was noted (in the Indian media) that 60 percent of the thermal coal power plants in India had less than seven days of stock because the rains had washed away the roads. And 30 percent of that 60 percent had less than one day of stock. They had reached critical levels due to the inadequacy of the infrastructure.

The third blocker to coal is quality. The quality of coal in India is poor; it has extremely high ash and sulfur content. For these three reasons coal has had difficulty in actually meeting its production targets, and indeed realizing perhaps the potential the policymakers had set out for it.

Oil is not available in abundance in India. India has 29 years of reserves-to-production ratio, but the bulk of these oil reserves are in areas that are geologically and topographically very complex. There is no easy oil left in India. It has been difficult to locate the oil, but it has been even more difficult to extract the oil on a commercial and sustainable basis.

Now, that does not mean that India hasn't had some successes. In the private sector, the Reliance Company discovered the world's largest gas fields in all of 2002, and it has a production potential of half a million barrels of oil equivalent (boe) today. There have been other smaller finds but they have all held out the expectation that India, in fact, has a large amount of reserves that have yet to be located. The problem is that these reserves are in very difficult terrain and it is not easy to access them.

India is hopeful about alternatives, but that is a long-term solution. Nuclear energy is very high on the agenda but, following Fukushima, there is local resistance. In early October 2011, a group of very senior ex-bureaucrats headed by a cabinet secretary filed a petition in the Supreme Court asking for a stay on all new nuclear generating plants. They also asked for a complete review of the safety conditions. The Supreme Court must look at this particular petition.

Wind Energy

India is currently producing 8 gigawatts (GW) of wind power and has, again on paper, huge expectations from wind. But here the problem lies with the site. It is never easy to actually locate a wind mill because of the need for land. Land rights in India have not been properly defined, title is never easily identified, and therefore it is not easy from a practical standpoint to actually expand or to scale up wind.

Solar Energy

Solar is the highest item on the prime minister's agenda. The government of India has given this great priority. But once again there are commercial, technical, and financial reasons why solar is unlikely to make a major impact on India's energy basket in the near future.

Biofuels

There is a lot of talk about biofuels. But every time a policy paper is written, it raises the issue of how do we reconcile the conflict between food and fuel.

The point is that while India has a broad base of energy resources, it is not able to extract the full potential from these resources, so supply is therefore struggling to keep pace with demand.

Technological Capacity

The third hard truth is that technology has been relatively underutilized or inefficiently utilized. The recovery rate of oil and gas from India's producing fields right now is 28 percent. This should be compared to an average recovery rate from fields of similar geology of around 40 percent. India's coal-based power plants have a converging factor of 30 percent, whereas the average in the world is about 37 percent. India has not actually managed to use technology that is available off the shelf in an efficient manner. It needs to do that.

Inadequate Policy Framework

The fourth hard truth is the absence of an institutional structure that allows for an integrated energy policy. As mentioned, India has seven or eight different ministries that are currently involved with energy. The consequence of that is the absence of one holistic framework within which an integrated energy policy can be framed.

Environmental Considerations

The final hard truth is that the environment is under stress. The link between economic growth, energy demand, and the environment is too strong, and we have not done enough to weaken this link. The fact is that the economy is almost totally reliant on fossil fuels. The fact is that gas, which is a relatively benign fossil fuel, has not yet achieved its position in the energy basket because of the absence of adequate distribution and logistics infrastructure. The fact is that 400 to 450 million people are currently using firewood and dung to meet their requirements. The indoor air pollution as a consequence of burning dung has led to respiratory illness that, according to the WHO, is one of the principal causes for premature death in India.

These are all very hard, hard truths, and India cannot even begin to address energy security issues if it does not tackle these hard truths. It cannot tackle these hard truths sequentially; it has to tackle them together. But in order for India to tackle these hard truths together, we have to recognize the issues, the constraints, the limitations within which the energy sector currently functions.

Intervening Issues

There is a set of internal conflicts that have a direct bearing on how energy policies are framed.

The first is the conflict between society and the state. India's society is vibrant, dynamic, and the people are demanding. They are questioning traditional concepts, they are upending traditional hierarchies, they are entrepreneurial, and they are clashing with a state that is still hesitant and suspicious of change. They are clashing with a state that has certainly shed its leftist rhetoric, but maybe they have not shed their leftist impulses.

This is a state that still wants to hold on to the energy sector. It has not unshackled the energy sector. It has not necessarily allowed the private sector and the government to operate on a level playing field. This is a clash between good economics and good politics. Good economics would demand that we must reduce subsidies. Good economics would suggest that we must use pricing as a countervailing factor to control demand, and that we must encourage real competition. Populist politics, good politics, however, fears the market. This clash between good politics and good economics is a major factor in the decisionmaking process regarding energy.

There is also a clash between centralization and federalization, or federalism. India is a federal polity. Energy is a central subject; it's a subject that is handled out of Delhi. But Delhi cannot implement its energy policy without the support of the state governments. It cannot implement its policy unless they have the support of governments that can give them access to lands. It cannot implement its policies if the political party in Delhi is in loggerheads with the political parties running the states. This dynamic between the center and the state is another factor that we need to keep in mind when we discuss the policy issues related to energy.

And finally, there is the dynamic between globalization and self-reliance. As mentioned, we are connected, but our oil sector today is aggressively looking for assets overseas. They already have a presence in 15 different countries. They are in partnership with a number of different international players. So they are looking aggressively to benefit from our connected and global world. But at the same time, the logic for going overseas is always written in a language that highlights national security or energy security. And sometimes this dynamic between the imperative of globalization and the imperative of nationalism, can actually lead to energy policy falling between the cracks.

Toward a National Energy Strategy

This is the backdrop against the next question: what should India's energy strategy then look like? Well, the premise of an energy strategy in India has to flow from the hard truths mentioned above. The fact is that fossil fuels will be the dominant fuel in India for the coming decades. The fact is that India must do something to weaken the link between economic growth, energy demand, and the environment. India has to also look at energy security against the short-term compulsions of ensuring that it does not suffer from technical and market disruptions, and the long-term requirement to ensure access to reliable and secure supplies. And India also has to premise its strategy on somehow moving the economy from fossil fuels toward the alternatives.

Those are the four premises upon which India's national strategy on energy should be based, and it is indeed the four premises upon which the government is currently looking to develop a national strategy. What should be the elements of this national strategy?

Boost Domestic Production and Smart Partnerships

There's no doubt that India has to do more to harness indigenous hydrocarbon fuels, its hydrocarbon resources. It has to not only bring technology that will improve the recovery rate from 28 percent to 40 percent or 45 percent, but must establish partnerships that will enable access to the oil and gas, and the new unconventionals like shale oil and shale gas that are certainly available in India but are difficult to locate and develop commercially. India cannot manage that on its own. It should be looking to liberalize coal mines so that the private sector has access to its coal mines. And it must certainly do more to ensure that the fiscal terms are competitive, are predictable, and there is no doubt in anyone's mind—whether the private sector, public sector, international or domestic—that contract terms will be respected, that it will not ex-post alter the terms that have been agreed to ex-ante.

Leverage Natural Gas Potential

The second element of India's strategy has to focus on natural gas. Natural gas is the bridge fuel between our present position and our hoped-for future situation when renewables become a more dominant part of the energy basket. The reason why natural gas has not acquired a more dominant position is because of the absence of pipelines, and also because India has not invested enough in liquid natural gas (LNG) port terminals. Now, both those facts are known to the government and both those facts are being considered aggressively by the government. There are plans to put up five more regasification terminals in the west coast of India, and there are plans to look at two LNG regas terminals in the east coast of India. A whole blueprint has been drawn up for a network that links the southern markets to gas supplies. Today, the two gas pipelines both cover the north and the west of India, but they do not go to the south. Gas is not available to the south of India. India has to do much more to accelerate the investment in infrastructure, to link the southern market to the gas-production system.

Rationalize Fuel Prices

The third important policy initiative, which has found expression in the Planning Commission report that is just being published, is to rationalize fuel prices. India just simply cannot afford to continue to subsidize petrol, diesel, kerosene, and LPG (liquefied petroleum gas). It is a burden on the exchequer; it makes a mockery of all hopes and plans to control India's fiscal deficits. But more than that, it is pushing the public-sector companies to the edge of Chapter 11 bankruptcy. It is also skewing the playing field between the public-sector companies and the private companies, and as a consequence the investment environment itself has been somewhat undermined.

Elevate Oil Diplomacy

There's an important reason for India now to elevate the role of its oil diplomacy. The bulk of its oil supplies come from the Middle East, and they come from Nigeria, and India will be reliant on those countries for years to come. India therefore has to see what can be done to better establish its relationship with the Middle East countries. They have oil production, India has the market. Perhaps there is scope here for upstream-downstream linkages. But, in effect, the idea of elevating the role of oil diplomats, energy diplomats, within India's policy framework is something that needs to find stronger traction.

Promote Demand Focus and Innovation

The demand conversation is a low-hanging fruit. It has not yet acquired the importance that it should have. As mentioned, there is no way India can meet its energy-security aspirations if it focuses only on the levers of supply. We have to also introduce demand into the equation. Demand conservation and energy efficiency has therefore got to be a very pivotal part of India's energy strategy. R&D expenditure is among the lowest in the industry. That has to change.

The technical-resource base in India is phenomenal. Shell, for instance, has a technical center in India; it is the only center of its kind east of Suez. At the time that Shell set up this center, it established a bar for short-listing candidates, and the bar had to be raised three times before Shell was able to start interviewing an acceptable number of people. There were far too many people who met the threshold that Shell had set out in the early stages of the center's development.

Today, Shell has 600 technocrat scientists and its own laboratory. They are providing support to the Shell Group of Companies around the world. Shell has decided to look at only three technology centers around the world, one of which will be the one set up in Bangalore. The reason for this example is to essentially highlight the fact that India has the human resource talent, but the industry has not spent enough on extracting the most from this talent. That is something that has to change.

Invest in Smart Infrastructure

India cannot push for an increase in the role of alternative energies unless it also invests heavily in smart infrastructure. India has wind farms in Tamil Nadu that are unable to actually provide energy because they have not been linked with the consumption centers. The fact is that India has to start looking at investments across the integrated alternative-energy value chain. It is no good just saying that we want to develop commercialized solar, wind, and biofuels. India has to also see what can be done to recalibrate its infrastructure so that these new forms of energy are able to meet the needs of the customer and are also able to be scaled up. That is one of the major impediments to developing new sources of energy in India. So the development and investment in smart infrastructure has to be a key element of strategy.

Increase U.S.-India Collaborations

India has to also now look at a much stronger collaboration with countries like the United States, and these collaborations must be in the realm of technology. Several examples have been mentioned regarding how technology can actually add value. Through the input of appropriate technology, India can shift the needle 5, 10, or 15 degrees, adding considerable value to the existing energy picture. India should not be looking at technology to radically reinvent the energy-consumption basket or the energy-supply situation, but the U.S. and India should look at technology to do better what we are already doing.

Establish a Super-Ministry on Energy

Finally, there's a need for a super-ministry in India that focuses on energy. India needs to actually ask the question: how does a country develop an energy policy if it is handled through a multiplicity of decisionmakers, each of whom have turf to protect, each of whom have companies to protect, and all of whom are looking at the energy picture through their particular silo? This issue perhaps is the most important and arguably the most urgent issue facing the Indian energy sector. Were India to create an institutional framework that allows for a more cohesive and integrated energy policy framework, it would be able to address many of these hard truths.

2 INDIA ON THE MOVE: INFRASTRUCTURE FOR THE 21ST CENTURY (PART I)

Remarks by Rajiv Lall, managing director and CEO, Infrasturcture Development Finance Company, Ltd., India

February 22, 2012

A Profile of the Indian Infrastructure Sector

Most people do not fully realize it, but what India has been trying to do in the infrastructure space is a direct consequence of, and a follow-on to, the reform process that was unleashed in 1991. The basic premise of the reform process was that we wanted to take away the so-called constraints of the so-called License Raj and enable, encourage, and unleash the potential of the fabled entrepreneurial energy that resides in India. And in many respects, across different sectors of the economy, that is what has happened.

Infrastructure is no exception. The political-speak for enabling private-sector participation in infrastructure is that this is a wonderfully dynamic thing and we really must have the private sector deliver these services. But the reality is that like many other parts of the world, the government does not have the resources to invest in the sector. After the fiscal consolidation of the 1990s that followed the reform program or that accompanied the reform program, we also saw an escalation in coalition politics.

And the economic or financial consequences of that evolution has been that progressively it has become much harder for the government of India to allocate any substantive, or really any, portion of its expenditures toward capital spending. And it is a declining line, which turned around only in 2002. The pressures of populist politics have, over time, deteriorated the composition of government expenditures, and that means that the government has had to rely very much on the private sector.

Starting in about 2002, the government made an effort to turn that trend around, even by means of government expenditure. But 2003 was the nadir of a 30- to 35-year period of spending on infrastructure, loosely defined as a share of GDP. This is in contrast to the years of the Indira Gandhi government and after, when a lot was being spent on rural infrastructure development and giving free power to farmers and others. That was the genesis of the Green Revolution in the 1970s and 1980s. It was only in 2003 that government expenditure on infrastructure started to increase. Between the 1980s and 2003, we came to about 3 percent of GDP equivalent of spending on infrastructure.

The last decade saw an extraordinary turnaround. And over this decade, spending on infrastructure, as a share of GDP, almost tripled from 3 percent of GDP to about 8 percent of GDP. What is remarkable is that in 2003, very little of that spending was a result of privately developed infrastructure. In 2008, roughly a third of that 8 percent was a result of private infrastructure. So private infrastructure is now doing approximately 3 percent of the GDP. So we are talking about $60 to $70 billion a year in private infrastructure. And when I say private infrastructure, I mean infrastructure where the equity risk is, in some measure, being taken by a private provider.

The scale of private participation is unprecedented in historical terms. And this is in sectors that are delivering services that are quasi-public goods. So whether it is electricity, water, transportation, or telecoms, there is an element of essential service that is being provided to the general consuming public.

My third comment is that private parties are being called upon to deliver these public services in a political context that is extraordinarily demanding. Whereas in the 19th century in the United States, private parties might have delivered infrastructure services, the expectations of the consuming public were very different. We did not even have universal suffrage then. In the 21st century, not only do we have universal suffrage, the expectations of the electorate are much higher than at any time before. Now electricity, access to water, and to communication and public transportation are increasingly considered to be part of people's rights. The sense of entitlement from the electorate is much, much higher than before.

India has reasonably strong institutions, but it is no secret that the administrative capacities of the government have been weakening over time and they are not as efficient as they used to be. We have a weak state apparatus whose dysfunction has been exacerbated because of the nature of our coalition politics.

If we juxtapose all four different aspects of the context—hugely increased, unprecedented participation of the private sector in the delivery of services that are regarded by a very active and politically conscious electorate as entitlements, within a weak state—this is a cocktail for an interesting rollercoaster ride. The intersection of public interest and public goods with private parties seeking to maximize profit is a well-known problem elsewhere in the world. It is challenging in most parts of the world. But when you transpose that into the Indian context, you can then understand the term "infrastruggles." It is a very, very difficult and challenging environment in which we are trying to deliver these services.

India's Achievements since 2003

First, there is port cargo-handling capacity, and this refers to container-handling capacity in particular, which is the modernization of port infrastructure. Over the last decade, capacity has tripled from 3 million twenty-foot equivalent units (TEU) to 9 million TEU. And the share of private participation has gone from under 25 percent to nearly 80 percent. Eighty percent of the current 9 million TEU are delivered through *privately* developed and privately managed ports.

Next is power generation, which is the subject of one of the two recent *Economist* articles. Today we have capacity of a little over 200,000 megawatts (MW), and we have added about 45,000 to 50,000 MW just over the last five years. It is short of the plan estimates or targets, but this is the most capacity we have added in any five-year period since independence.

And what is more extraordinary is that of the 200,000 MW of current capacity, roughly 30 percent is actually in private hands—privately developed and privately managed. There's another 20,000 MW of capacity that is currently under construction for completion in the next fiscal year, and two-thirds of that is private. So by the end of the next fiscal year, we will have close to 220,000 or 230,000 MW in operation, of which more than a third will be in private hands.

There is also the telecoms story, which has been the poster child of Indian infrastructure, and is well known to many. In just over the last decade we have gone from under 20 million subscribers to close to 950 million subscribers. Two-thirds of these subscribers are urban; one-third is rural. Urban penetration is 160 percent now and rural penetration is close to 40 percent. The cost of telecom service delivery has come down from 15 rupees per minute, or 30 U.S. cents, to 1.5 U.S. cents per minute.

That is the scale and speed with which this bit of infrastructure has been built. We have paved about 13,000 kilometers of new roads. The previous minister used to boast that he would bid up to 20 kilometers a day of new roads for private participation. We are now up to 15 kilometers a day, so over 13,000 kilometers of road have been bid out for private participation.

It is the largest public-private partnership (PPP) program currently in operation anywhere in the world. In absolute terms the numbers, compared to China, are nothing. But in terms of the scale of private participation, and in the Indian context, these numbers are absolutely humungous.

Analyzing the State of the Indian Infrastructure Sector

The successes within Indian infrastructure reaffirm and revalidate that the execution capacity and risk-taking capacity of our entrepreneurs is indeed phenomenal. The quality of what has been built, whether it is new roads, power plants, or ports, has been excellent. And the efficiency per gantry crane is as high as Singapore.

Almost all of this is domestically funded. So it demonstrates that our financial system, notwithstanding its limitations and frailties, has had the depth and the breadth, so far, to accommodate this huge expansion.

Furthermore, the success of the infrastructure sector shows the depth and breadth of the supporting ecosystem to make all of this happen. You need a whole bunch of professionals that are able to write the contracts and enforce the contracts, because these are complex commercial arrangements, and that ecosystem does exist in India.

And finally, the success demonstrates that there must have been some government policy breakthroughs to enable all of this. It is not as if government policy is completely dysfunctional. Without some initial breakthroughs, we would not have had the pace of development that we have had.

However, there is also a downside. Imagine a car that must have four wheels. One wheel is government. The second wheel is the private sector. The third wheel is civil society, and the fourth wheel is regulators and judiciary.

For this whole system to keep working, for this car to keep rolling, all wheels must be riding or turning at the same speed. What has happened in the last decade is that the private-sector wheel of this car has gotten ahead of itself.

After years of repression, years of suppression of this huge entrepreneurial energy, finally in the 1990s, the bottle was uncorked. The genie came out of it. The hugely enthusiastic private sector that is driven by profit emerges and they invest left, right, and center and they have created this huge stock of investment.

But the wheel that is government is not turning quite as fast. There is weak administrative capability. And what that means in this context is that there is room for gaming.

The civil-society wheel that has been dormant for some time becomes more vocal when they realize the government and the private sector are not really in sync. So now there is systematic protest. You have civil-society movements that are becoming more and more articulate, vociferous, and influential, aided by a very effective media.

And this is between the middle class and the media. The media in our country is privately owned and the commercial interests of the media lie with the middle class because that is where advertising dollars are generated. So anything of concern to the middle class gets amplified in the media, especially the electronic media. And corruption has become a big issue for the middle class in India. It has been picked up by the media and amplified.

So when all this is happening, the regulators and the judiciary are compelled to react. And it is a blunt instrument, let's face it. I am now referring pointedly to the Supreme Court decision on revoking the 122 telecom licenses. Morally and ethically it was the right thing to do, it is a correct judgment. But it has consequences for business. There are some people who entered into the contracts on the presumption that they were valid contracts. Now those contracts have been declared invalid. What does it do to the billions of dollars the Norwegians invested in Indian telecom?

There are five areas where there is a lot of work to be done.

Five Areas to Develop

Land

The first is the acquisition of land when it comes to developing infrastructure. Land is a hugely emotive issue in our country. It is very scarce, and it is at the heart of distributive justice. So when fat cats come acquire land, using the state as a shield, supposedly acquiring land for the public purpose, and the public sees that this land is being used to generate profits, it causes some reaction, rightly or wrongly.

This is a grey area. If I acquire land for a power project to generate electricity for the public, I can argue quite legitimately it is for the public purpose. But if I have a captive mine associated with that, a captive coal mine, which gives me extraordinary profits, then the debate could swing the other way.

How we distribute land and what is fair is one set of issues. But what is efficacious is quite another set of issues. The political system is such that we are focused on fairness, but efficiency is being relegated to a second-order debate. In the world of political rhetoric, efficiency of decision-making does not figure.

The legislation that is being proposed today is potentially disastrous from the point of view of business, but it has the perception of being *fair*. This is a huge challenge that needs to be addressed, and land is at the heart of it.

Environment

The environment is a similar issue. It mostly has to do with deforestation and water. It just so happens that most of our coal lies in heavily forested areas of the country, where most of our tribal communities also live. When access is given to mining companies, trees are cut down and people are displaced.

How do you find the balance between the rights of those individuals and the obvious need for coal? We have 280 billion tons of coal reserves. We have the fifth-largest coal reserves anywhere in the world, but we cannot dig it out of the ground to feed our power plants. And the environment is at the center of that big fight.

Financing

Financing for public infrastructure is very easy; it is just budgetary financing. But private financing for private projects is much more complex. It requires the layering of differing kinds of securities and other complicated procedures.

There is a mismatch between the savings that we have, where they lie, and the needs of the infrastructure sector. It is not as if we do not have significant savings, we save 35 percent of GDP.

The bulk of those savings lies in banks or is not properly intermediated through the formal financial system. And so they are not available with a long-enough term that can be delivered to infrastructure, because the long terms must match the long term of the assets.

There is a mismatch that requires institutional evolution. We need to develop our own pension and insurance industry, which is happening but will take time. Today we have a disconnect, so we have to rely on a bridging mechanism, on long-term savings from overseas. And we have to find creative solutions, and this is where connectivity with the U.S. capital markets in particular is very important to us.

Administrative Capacity

The fourth issue that we need to resolve is administrative capacity. Coal India is an example. Today we are importing 50 million tons of coal per year at a cost of $5 billion, whereas we have all the coal in the world. And we are not able to do it because Coal India has been singularly unprepared for the pace at which generating plants have come on-stream. They have never seen this in 50 years.

There is 30,000 to 40,000 MW of new capacity suddenly coming up; although they have promised that they will provide coal, they just do not have the ability to do it. The situation is completely suboptimal because we do not have the administrative capacity to bring the coal out of the ground in time. We are going to have to rely on imported coal at triple the price, the cost of which will have to be borne eventually by the taxpayer.

Regulation

And finally, we need to vastly improve our regulatory capability, because regulation in this intersection between private and public, which is so intense in India, has to be absolutely first rate. They have to adjudicate between the interests of the risk-taking private provider of the service and the general public good. The regulatory community has been politically influenced, and do not have the capacity and the sophistication to stand up independently from government and make those regulatory decisions.

The Great Muddle-Through

Finally, let me turn to the way forward. Roads and airports are still doing reasonably well. But the two big sectors, telecoms and power, are reeling from this: the wheels of this car are going in different directions. Going forward, it could be characterized as "The Great Muddle-Through."

We have to live with third- or fourth-best policy choices. And while there can be no accommodation for corruption, let me describe to you the real-life dilemma of a sincere public official called upon to make critical decisions. The choice for a number of public officials is either to have no infrastructure, candidly admitting to the lack of administrative capacity within government to deliver it, or to tolerate some untidiness in the system and have infrastructure built.

Here is an example in the telecom sector. The comptroller and auditor general, who has acted as a very strong voice of conscience on the telecom issue, estimated the loss from the manner in which the 122 telecom licenses were given out. The last set of telecom licenses were given out at close to $35 billion. He is trying to make a rhetorical point, to bring this issue to the center of public debate.

Depending upon how you discover the price of spectrum, I estimate the real cost lost to the exchequer to be closer to $10 to $15 billion, and not $35 billion. Ten billion dollars is less than what we spend on our food subsidies. And of those food subsidies it has been empirically recorded that two-thirds to three-quarters are wasted. They do not even get to the intended recipient.

The telecom companies that got licenses even in 2001 have not made beyond-normal profits—only $2 revenue per user per month; 1.4 cents per minute is really not a profit. It is hypercompetitive. Why are we debating this issue to the extent that we are? We must go after corruption, but we have to keep perspective. The debate has gotten out of hand, and we are losing sight of the more important things that we have to achieve.

So in "The Great Muddle-Through," I suspect what will happen is that there will be an accommodation whereby deals will be cut and in the power sector, for example, power purchase agreements that were supposed to be binding for 25 years will have to be reviewed, and will be allowed to pass through the higher cost of imported coal—which means that lenders will be protected. The asset will be built. The equity returns for the developer will decrease, but the cost to the consumer will increase.

So the pain will be distributed somewhat widely, and there will be debate about how fair that distribution of the pain has been. But it will be a "muddle-through" because the ideal situation would be that we get our act together in Coal India and mine the coal that we are sitting on at a third of the cost, and use that to fire our power plants rather than relying on imported coal from Australia at three times the price. So that is the "muddle-through" in power.

A similar story will unfold in telecoms, where the aggrieved parties will come back to the table, and probably bid again. They will have to absorb some higher cost, but they will be allowed to operate. There will be some consolidation in the industry and life will go on. And I can go on from sector to sector, but that is the nature of the "muddle through" that is likely to manifest itself.

Now you can ask, Is that good enough? Is the best we can do, in the complex country that we are, a "muddle-through" in the construction of such an important sector? And the answer is surely no. A "muddle-through" cannot be good enough.

The Challenges Ahead

What are the challenges for the next 10 years? For the next 10 years, we have to deal with the challenge of urbanization. That is going to be the next big wave for infrastructure. We expect over the next 20 years, our urban population will grow by 250 to 300 million people. There will be about 600 million to 650 million people living in cities in India by 2030. The quality of our cities is deteriorating by the day. The administrative capacity to plan urban infrastructure does not exist. The fiscal base for our towns is nonexistent. How is this infrastructure going to be built?

Water is only now beginning to appear on the edges of the debate. We are depleting our water table at an astonishing rate. I will conclude by leaving you with one fact about water: we have been subsidizing the use of electricity for irrigation pumps for the longest time. And government after government makes the supply of electricity to farmers free. Pump irrigation is what is causing our water tables to deplete at an astonishingly fast rate.

What was intended to help agriculture production has become a huge problem in terms of availability of water resources. And the politics of it is such—and this is the fundamental issue with democracies—that we are unable to think about the long term. So, how we start focusing on the long term and translate that into political decisions today, I think that is the challenge we are facing in all capitalist democracies. And we are no different, except that we are at a different stage of our evolution.

However, I am hopeful. And the reason I am hopeful is that I think that we are on the cusp of a radical change in the nature of politics in our country. And it is the youth, urbanization, the growth of the middle class and media that are conspiring to bring about that change.

A young demographic and urbanization, combined with electoral reform, means that the concerns being expressed through the electorate will become more issue-based rather than identity-based. The dynamics of the middle class and media will begin to exert huge pressure and influence that will change policies. And hopefully a combination of those two forces will help us navigate the challenges that lie ahead.

Thank you.

3 INDIA ON THE MOVE: INFRASTRUCTURE FOR THE 21ST CENTURY (PART II)

Remarks by John L. Flannery, president and CEO, General Electric (GE) India

July 6, 2012

GE has been in India in one form or another for 110 years. Amazingly, someone ventured out in 1902 from the United States and came to India and built a hydroelectric power plant, and no one can account for who that was or why they came to India in 1902, but it was built in Karnataka and GE has been in the country commercially ever since then.

Between 1993 and 2000, GE built up a lot of back-office presence in India, and was one of the first companies to develop the business process outsourcing (BPO)—and you now know that company as Genpact. GE did the same thing with many research and development and engineering activities in Bangalore, so today there are 5,000 scientists, engineers, and others doing work for GE in Bangalore. That was a big phase of GE's development in India and it was trailblazing.

In the last three years we have been trying to make the company much more commercial. GE India still has back-end activities, but is now much more commercial and especially more local. GE India is now a stand-alone local company with products and manufacturing in India, which is a change from the way we have done things in the past.

The large sectors that GE is involved in are:

Energy: GE is heavily involved in power generation; renewable energy, specifically the wind business; digital energy, and water-related treatment.

Health care: Health care is a very large and strongly growing business for us in India; mostly imaging equipment and related services.

Transportation: GE makes aircraft engines, locomotive engines, and all the related services that would go with that.

And lastly, GE Capital: In addition to day-to-day financing, GE Capital finances a number of infrastructure projects. Quite often we might put equity into a project or development company that is also working with GE on the commercial side. GE therefore has a pretty wide-ranging view of the activity in the infrastructure sector in India right now. Overall, we've got about 15,000 employees in the country.

The global economic scenario right now really touches India and the infrastructure space in particular in a few ways. GE, as you know, is thought of as an American company in many ways, but our number-one strategic commitment is to grow the company outside of the United States.

Currently 62 percent of our total sales come from outside of the United States. So GE has a very broad international footprint that keeps growing.

Our economic outlook for the United States right now is basically flat. It is not in crisis mode, but there is not a lot of economic activity in the United States. Our outlook on Europe is that it is very weak and will continue to be so for the next couple of years. As for China, GE is quite positive—we are of the view that China has many options to manage through the current economic situation. They are transitioning their broad macroeconomy from being a pure or heavily export-dependent one into more of a domestic-consumption model. The outlook for China is pretty stable, with decent growth, and not the precipitator of global crisis, as others would have it.

I would say one common theme across all these markets and India right now is jobs. Jobs are a massive issue for every country around the world. They are very keenly invested in trying to create and retain jobs, and in that context there is also a very raw sense of fairness (or unfairness) in many of these countries right now. This is a very dynamic debate and has ramifications for issues on trade policy and income distribution. This is the global context in which India is being assessed today by investors—both financial investors and businesses like GE. And the factors around how these other economies are doing does affect India in certain ways.

One of the critical things for India and for any country to do is recognize that infrastructure is a lynchpin and of vital importance to the economy. It is not just one of 10 things that a government needs to work on; we view it as number one, two, or three, after national security. And infrastructure really is "a gift that keeps on giving." You get many, many benefits from investing in infrastructure, both short term and long term. So it really is a critical asset and attribute of a country. And alternatively, lack of investment can really starve an economy of basic strength.

We urge countries and policymakers to really put this issue on a level that's quite separate from the dozen other different issues they grapple with—that infrastructure is really a critical issue. Secondly, look at infrastructure in a positive way, in a sense that it means a lot more opportunity for countries. In a number of markets people view it as a hassle, as a negative thing. But it really is a very positive opportunity for a country. You get a significant amount of jobs and investment in the short term from the project themselves, and then long-term productivity for the economy from the aftermath of these projects.

So in the context of infrastructure being critical and critically important, I will talk a little bit about the energy infrastructure business in India right now, which is not a particularly positive story. And in the sense of criticality, we would like to see some changes.

Good News, Bad News Story

Energy infrastructure in India is a "good news, bad news" story. The bad news is that many agree that India only really reacts in the face of a crisis. And the good news is that in energy, we absolutely have a crisis right now. This is not an academic issue in any sense; there are very tangible things happening on the ground.

An energy business has three basic components: one is the power generation itself; second is transmitting it and distributing it across the country; and then the third is the price of power. And in India at this point, there are major problems across the whole continuum.

First, in power generation, there is a significant and growing shortage of power. Ten to 13 percent shortages are roughly accurate, but they are rapidly expanding. There have been no large-scale gas or coal-powered projects done in the last year, and probably almost 18 months. There are issues around fuel, the supply of natural gas, the availability of coal, and the price of coal. But in the power-generation side of the industry today, there are major shortfalls. In our own customer base, there are between 5 and 6 gigawatts of completed power projects that are not operating due to lack of fuel. To put that in perspective, that is roughly the energy supply for the Delhi metro area. These multibillion-dollar investments are basically stranded for lack of fuel supply.

Second, the distribution network is very troubled in a couple of ways. One is the efficiency of the network—it is referred to as a "lost percentage," and is very high in India. There is a large gap between the percentage of electricity that is generated and what is ultimately paid for: this is leakage, in one sense, and theft, in many circumstances. India would be quite high in any global ranking of the dissipation of power production to actual consumption of it. And that has created a lot of financial stress in the distribution companies. Today most of them (and arguably all of them) are financially stressed at a minimum, or altogether financially unviable, whether through excessive debt or inability to make payments.

Those are the major issues in power generation and distribution. Ultimately that translates to the fact that tariff rates have to increase. If you step back and wonder whether the energy business is viable from A to Z, you cannot say that about energy in India today.

The GDP growth rate that came out in the last quarter—5.3 percent—was an interesting number. We had been pretty bearish on GDP in India over the last few quarters, mostly from watching our own customers and our own portfolio, and watching our own levels of activities and orders. But one of the things in particular we were seeing was how the energy sector was affecting other parts of the Indian economy. For example, in some of our supply chains, a lot of customers were coming to us saying that, while in the newspaper it is called load shedding or a power holiday (or some other innocuous-sounding term), "I don't have power three days a week. I can't turn my plant on and off every other day and have a viable business." While it is difficult to determine exactly how much of India's GDP contraction is power-related, I would argue that it is a significant amount and that the trend will probably accelerate in the next quarter or two.

So the bottom line is that the power business is in a "best of times, worst of times" situation. It is a fundamentally attractive space and will continue to be, but it has some issues in the short term.

Recommendations

Change the Mindset

First, and most significantly, change in the mindset is more important than a change in the policies. But if I had to pick just one—if policies are implemented and acted on in a timely manner, in general they can work. Yes, there are issues around land acquisition, et cetera; there are a number of policies that could be better. What we see right now is a lack of implementation of existing policies.

We have expressed our concern with the lack of urgency, what we call a "man on the moon mentality," which demands picking a certain number of projects and focusing on them. In the last few weeks I have been encouraged; the prime minister's office and the planning commission have started an attempt at ring-fencing a number of projects—15 to 20 projects that they feel have got to get done. But this should be replicated in the rest of the country, with a sense of unity—forget the political squabbling, forget the opposition. We have got to get into a mode where people agree that for the common good of the country, the economy, every person in the country, certain things just have to happen. I think a mindset change is needed to get a few deals under way.

Another example is the locomotive business; GE has been waiting for years for a tender to invest in locomotive production. It is shovel-ready—if the government pushed a button tomorrow, there would be people showing up to make proposals, to invest hundreds of millions (and more) in India to build factories and to create jobs. The people are ready to go if [the government] could just clear the debris and get them going.

One thing you would see is that the mood would snap back extremely quickly. As depressed and negative as sentiment has been in the last three to six months, I think you would find that just the sense that there are a couple of projects underway would have a very profound impact on business confidence and business conditions in the country. Again, that is less of a policy change and more of a can-do attitude. In the last few weeks we have seen some more of that, and I hope that is a trend that continues.

Long-term Financing

In terms of specific policies that would benefit from change, one is long-term financing. These projects—whether a road, port or a power plant—have a long-term horizon. Ten to 30 years might be the time frame for financing. It's quite risky for a developer to take two-, five-, seven-year loans and have to risk the availability or cost of financing.

It is not an insurmountable issue. Even with the constraints around financing today, we still see a lot of people willing to do projects if they could get them permitted and green-lighted. There is a basic shortage of long-term financing, but there is no shortage of suggestions: whether it is allowing pension funds and other long-term pools of capital to invest in infrastructure. There are plenty of remedies, but progress on this issue is critical. It would facilitate the magnitude of investment in India.

Tax Policy

The tax policies of India need a very serious reexamination, and I think the prime minister made some references to that in the last few days. As bullish as we are on India long term, we were concerned and disturbed by some of the proposals in the tax components of the budget in March. These are things that do not sound like they are directly related to infrastructure, but they are closely related to the mindset of investors and the risks that they perceive about the country.

For example, the retroactive tax in particular sent shockwaves through GE at the highest levels, and I think many other companies felt the same way. Without even debating the peculiarities of the tax codes, the reaction was that there is a willingness to change the basic rules of the game well after the game has started, and there is an apparent willingness to circumvent or overrule the Supreme Court. One of the hallmarks of India for investors all along has been that it is a fair place to do business. It may take time to get things through the judicial system, but you know what the law is; the law is ultimately applied in a way that you can rely on.

We met with a number of people in the government to explain that they should at least understand the potential ramifications of this particular route, in that a lot of investors will likely pull their money out of India—financial investors in particular. And as a result, there will be a lot of pressure on the currency of the country right away. That unfortunately has happened, and we hope to see some of those things addressed in a different fashion.

To summarize, GE is a long-term investor in India, has been here for a long time, and have significant investments in the country. We continue to increase our investments in the country. So we are fundamentally big fans of India – we have a big, bullish view on India especially in the infrastructure space.

With the right mindset being broadly adopted across government, multinational companies, and Indian companies—that [infrastructure] is a critical space for the country to support, that it has very clear short-term and long-term benefits for the country and just getting to this implementation mentality—we think there is going to be a lot of upside and quick rebound. For all the back-and-forth on the issue, companies still have lots of interest in investing in India. And I think we would all be surprised at the degree to which this thing can bounce back from where the gloom is today.

4 THE UNITED STATES AND INDIA: INNOVATING HEALTH CARE

Remarks by Pratap C. Reddy, chairman, Apollo Hospitals Group, India

July 24, 2012

All of us know that there is no country where there are no pinpoints in health care, with respect to the most advanced countries or developing countries like India or the underdeveloped countries. But briefly, Indian health care today is what it was in the United States 20 years ago. But then there is a difference. Some institutions in the country are on par with some of the best facilities available anywhere in the world, including the United States, and others are not. Indian health care challenges are major.

The first major challenge is that we have inadequate hospital beds. There is one hospital bed for 1,050 people. In the United States there is one hospital bed for 250 people. In Japan, it's luxurious; they have one bed for 80 people. To bridge this gap, we have been telling the government that we need to add 1,100 beds per year for the next decade, at a cost of billions of rupees.

The second challenge that we have is something you will not believe: despite having 385 million people below the age of 30, India does not have an adequate supply of health human resources. Rather than a challenge, I will say this should be an opportunity to develop these health human resources. If you take the number of doctors or nurses and compare with the United States, we are at least at five times a disadvantage. We need to augment the doctor-nurse force and paramedicals several times over. A country should automatically look at this and say, here is an opportunity to provide jobs.

There are several well-meaning organizations that have been pushing the government to encourage, not regulate, health human resources development. We have done this at Apollo; we have 56 hospitals and 11 nursing colleges. But we feel this is inadequate and want to double our efforts. We currently train about 3,000 to 4,000 paramedics and others. We feel there is opportunity to double and triple this, to take it to 30,000 to 40,000 per year.

Year after year, the Confederation of Indian Industry (CII) has been submitting memorandums to the Ministry of Health, the Ministry of Finance, and others. We have requested them to give health and education national priority, and we are starting to see that happen. Fourteen years ago, when the government gave the IT industry and infrastructure a "priority status," there was significant development because it was seen as contributing to the national economy. It has contributed to creating jobs. I think that will happen several times more if only health and education are given national priority status.

Unfortunately, you and I know the governments are not doing it because they feel it is the obligation of the government to educate and provide health care for its people, although they have realized that they cannot. Even in advanced countries like the United States, we all know how much it costs the government to provide health care or education for everyone.

It is not a tax loss—it is a big gain to the government. Everybody has great expectations that reforms will happen under the dynamic prime minister in the month of September. I think this is essential in order to take the next leap in providing adequate health care, by having an adequate number of people to man the system.

The third major challenge is frightening. India has had infectious diseases before, and fortunately some of the major ones like plague and cholera have been controlled. The World Health Organization (WHO) recently noted that India is probably free of polio. That is because of the government's efforts to undertake a massive immunization program. But India still has a 40 percent rate of death occurring from communicable or infectious diseases.

We need to rapidly address this issue by way of adequate prevention and vaccination. India is proud that its vaccination companies are producing enormous amount of vaccines. Last year the industry was valued at about $900 million; they export 40 percent of their product. UNICEF is one of the main sources through which 100 countries in the rest of the world benefit from the vaccines produced in India. The other day, I met an entrepreneur in Hyderabad who said he is going to make a vaccine to prevent Hepatitis C that would cost a few cents a shot! But what we need is greater thrust in the development of health care human resources so that we can meet the challenges of preventable communicable and infectious diseases.

But a larger issue that India and other Asian countries are facing is noncommunicable diseases (NCDs). You are all aware the UN had the first summit on noncommunicable diseases last May. As far as India is concerned, tomorrow the 2012 Olympics start, and we all want to win a gold medal. But India has already won three gold medals—we are the diabetic capital of the world, cancer capital of the world, and heart disease capital of the world.

On diabetes—whatever numbers were talked about in 2000 were far exceeded by 2010. By 2020 we expected that there would be 36 million Indians with diabetes, but by 2011 the statistics reveal that we have already crossed the 75 million-mark, and it is estimated that one out of every five diabetics in the world will be an Indian.

As for heart disease, I am a cardiologist. The entire concept of Apollo came because I was a practicing cardiologist, but when patients needed surgery, there were not adequate facilities in India—I used to send my patients abroad. One of those days, I lost a young man. He was only 38 years old, leaving behind a 31-year-old wife and two small children. And you know why? He couldn't raise $50,000 to come to the United States for care. I looked at that and said, how many more families are going to face this tragedy? That is the vision of Apollo, to bring quality health care to reach the various cross-sections of our people.

I think we have succeeded because we have the same quality outcomes as any hospital anywhere in the world. It was hard, but we have done 130,000 coronary bypass surgeries, and our outcomes are the same as the best institutions anywhere in the world. What we are happy about is that for the lower-income group, we charged $3,000 on day one, and it still costs them only $3,000 for a coronary by-pass surgery. The outcome is still 99 percent-plus, but this is still only available to a limited amount of the population.

In these three diseases—diabetes, cancer, and heart disease—we should work as a unified group, and not just in India. In health, we all accept the great developments that took place in the United States in technology for diagnosis, in methodologies, in research, in new innovations—in all of these, there are great institutions in this country that have done enormous work and continue to do a lot of research and innovation.

This is where I think we need to take the huge resources that are available, and where the rest of the world should work. The WHO, World Bank, and governments of the 50 to 70 countries that have acute problems in health care could work together to find a common solution.

What are the new tools that are available, and how do we get them to our patients? How can information technology (IT) be used to transform delivery of health care? Recently in Heidelberg, there was a conference attended by the "Who's Who" around the world transforming health care using IT. Everybody was saying we have all these tools and we can bring this together. At Apollo, we believe that we should change health care delivery—integrating health care from the hospital to the clinic to the home using IT. If we can do that, I can instantly release 70 percent of the beds at Apollo and make them available for more critical patients.

This is no longer a dream. We need to be able to benefit from each other's help. For example, in the United States there are electronic medical records (EMRs). The rest of the world could have these, too. Indian companies have helped create EMRs—including our own company, Apollo Health Street. Why shouldn't the rest of the world now do this? We must pool our resources to make this happen.

There are so many wonderful innovations coming from the research happening in every single field in the West. I know what is happening in Europe, and the many things that are happening in great institutions in the United States. We need to take this and not reinvent it, in order to benefit millions of people.

I think we also need a more holistic approach. Apollo has a CSR [corporate social responsibility] program called the Billion Hearts Beating (BHB). We have the BHB campaign in order to reach people and say that you do not have to die at 30 of a heart attack, or suffer the complications of diabetes, or get cancer just to be fashionable by smoking, control your diabetes and hypertension, and most importantly, we should use the relaxation techniques that we have exported to the West—yoga and meditation.

Several of these things will make a significant difference and some of those ancient medicines are still available for many ailments. China also has a tremendous amount of ancient medicine. We should look at using ancient medicine, and see how they can bring a more holistic approach to health care. This is what I think we can give back to the United States—you are the most advanced country in everything, including health care, but what is needed is to include some of these methods that have no side effects and are less expensive. You do not have to spend 15 percent of U.S. GDP on health care.

Recently the Indian government increased the GDP expenditure on health care from 1 to 2.5 percent. It is a very small amount, which probably will not even help our inflation or help us renovate the various medical facilities in our country. But we must admire that they did something.

It is a great honor to be here with you. I could go on speaking about our problems, but I can speak with greater enthusiasm because the problem is solvable. But how can it be solved? India cannot solve it. The United States cannot solve it. You and I cannot solve it. But together, we can solve it. If we do it together, we will have transformed not only today's health care but have given back for the next few generations of good health. IT is going to make a big difference. We need to give it the full potential to make the transformation to better health for a lot of people.

5 THE UNITED STATES, INDIA, AND THE FUTURE OF AUTOMOTIVE MANUFACTURING

Remarks by Arvind Goel, president & head, Business Group, Tata Autocomp Systems Ltd

December 12, 2012

Editor's Note: Selected slides from Arvind Goel's presentation can be found in Appendix A. For the full PowerPoint presentation, please visit the following CSIS web page: https://csis.org/event/emerging-indian-economy-signature-speaker-series-future-manufacturing.

It is expected that the Indian economy should grow next year at a rate of 6 percent; this year it has come down close to 5 percent. India really needs 7 percent-plus growth to sustain its growth on a long-term basis and to keep employment rates steady.

There is a lot of negativity in the international market because the growth rate in India fell in the last couple of quarters, and it has come down to 5.3 percent. But as the fundamentals of the economy are strong, it will come back. People who want to invest in India should look at the far longer-term perspective rather than looking at a short-term perspective. India is only a 1.7-trillion-dollar economy today, but it is growing fast, and it is expected that by 2022 India should be among the largest economies in the world.

Of the 15 top global manufacturers in 1980, China was the 7th position and has moved to 2nd position by 2010. India, from 15th position, has moved to 10th, not because growth has been extremely good, but because other countries' growth did not meet expectations.

The purpose of discussing this is that there is a huge scope for India to grow, with its large population and technically skilled workers. Another slide shows the top 10 global innovators for the local market; here, China has been really doing extremely well, and India is far behind.[1] A lot of training and activities for innovation are happening in India, and we expect this to improve over time.

It is important from the Indian long-term perspective that the manufacturing sector grows at a much higher pace because there is a huge number of young people who seek work, and unless the manufacturing sector grows, there can be huge social problems in the country. So, there has been a strong focus by the government for a manufacturing policy, which I will explain later as well.

As you see from this slide, in the manufacturing sector the CAGR [compound annual growth rate] has been only 8.7 percent in totality, in spite of the automotive sector's CAGR of nearly 15 percent.[2] The CAGR in the automotive sector is expected to grow at a much larger pace. For 2013

1. See slide 1 in Appendix A.
2. See slide 2 in Appendix A.

it may slightly slow down because of this year's low GDP growth, so the investments into manufacturing have fallen short. But on a long-term perspective, the automobile sector is making huge investments. So, the CAGR growth in the automotive sector looks very attractive, and this will follow in the other manufacturing industries as well, due to government policies.

The manufacturing sector's contribution to employment is critical for economic growth, as it employs 12 percent of the country's labor force. Unless this grows to a level closer to 20 percent in next 10 years, there will be huge unemployment issue in the country. So there has been a massive push by industry and the government so that the manufacturing industry grows, with a particular focus on the labor-intensive industries.

High inflation is one of the biggest challenges that India faces today; currently it stands at about 8 to 9 percent. Industrial output is contracting after sustained monetary tightening and higher credit costs, so the cost of capital has gone up because inflation has gone up. Capital is more expensive because interest rates are up—and so as always, industry is watching to invest at the right time, when the interest rates are reasonably okay. But large companies, including the house of Tata, have always thought that we need to invest well in time and not wait for the time to come. You have to create your own time, and you need to leapfrog.

How does India fare in a comparison of factors affecting competitiveness in low-cost countries? [This refers to] different factors of design and engineering skill, manufacturing skills, manpower cost, domestic demand, commercial environment, supplier base, raw-material infrastructure. [The] key point is that the commercial environment in India should be improved, and that is where a lot of work has recently been done. India is more competitive than most low-cost countries except China and the Czech Republic. India is more competitive in manufacturing costs, manufacturing skills, local-market size, and the established supplier base. A vast amount of supplies are available across the country and India has a huge amount of manpower. The critical issue is the training of this manpower to fit specific needs.

Another challenge facing the sector is the rising cost of labor. With the cost of manpower going up, the cost of labor in India is now about $1.40 an hour, as compared to China, which is at $1.80 an hour. We have a plant in China where costs are even higher: if an international investor is investing into these countries, the workers expect larger amounts of money to be paid.

How does India compare on inputs like the cost of power, rising labor wages, and tariffs? Slide 24 shows these comparisons among various countries, and India is really at the highest level—expensive?—close to Japan and Germany.[3] Similarly, the labor wages in India are higher than some of these countries. India really lags behind on the cost of capital, and is on the highest side of the borrowing interest rates and the raw-material prices.

The constraints in material flow is one of the key challenges in India, and a lot of international players, from the United States or Europe or Japan, when they put their plants in India, cite infrastructure—roads, rail, coal supply chain—as one of the key issues that they face. If a truck moves goods from Bombay to Delhi, it needs to stop at 12 places because of infrastructure or the local laws. The government of India is putting a lot of emphasis on the Golden Quadrilateral, the Bombay-Delhi industrial corridor, and also standardizing state taxes so that the business becomes easier to conduct across state borders.

---

3. See slide 3 in Appendix A.

India will need about 200 million to 250 million additional jobs over the next 15 years to employ the children currently in school. The demographic dividend will come from the flow of these children in the workforce. This requires an education policy consistent with the country's changing needs. There have been lengthy discussions between policymakers in Delhi and industry, and a lot of the education is now getting structured between technical institutes and skill-development centers so that skills are developed for the respective industry. The key is to grow and to create skills in the country, and I think on both these counts there has been a tremendous amount of work going on.

Land reform is still a major issue, but I am not sure how soon it will get resolved, even though a lot of work is going on in this direction. Tata Motors recently had a major issue when it put a plant in an economic zone in West Bengal. The local politicians had issues, and later we had to ship the plant to Gujarat, which is a more [business] friendly state. These hiccups do happen, but negative news spreads fast. Tata Motors has put thousands of plants all over the country, but they had problems only in one plant. In the other few thousand plants, there was no news. So, there are issues around land acquisition, but things are moving in the right direction.

India today produces about 3 million passenger cars per year, and in 2020, it is expected to do 10 million. I am also on the executive committee of SIAM, which is the Society of Indian Automobile Manufacturers, and we recently had an executive committee meeting. It was unanimously agreed that in spite of the GDP rate dropping in the last two quarters—and it's not likely to grow for the next couple of quarters to the extent we want—on a long-term basis, we still want to keep the same figure.

Slide 36: This shows the quantum of growth that will happen in the commercial-vehicle sector, from nearly 1 million to 2.35 million.[4] It's not only the number that is growing at this pace; the tonnage of the trucks would also increase. Much larger-tonnage trucks are coming into place. So the value of these commercial vehicles, if they increase the volume, is going from 1 million to 2.3 million; by value terms, it is much larger than what the growth is. Similarly, the tractor and two-wheeler segments are expected to grow rapidly—the production of two-wheelers is likely to touch 20 million by 2020. And even construction vehicles, which are usually imported but are now being made domestically, have started growing.

There is a huge quantum of opportunity and possibility in the automotive industry. And the automotive industry is not the only one—it also goes for the component industry, the service industry, and the dealerships. There is a long chain of employment involved in the whole industry. Today, the automotive industry makes up 8 percent of the manufacturing sector, and it's likely to go to almost 20 percent toward the total manufacturing industry in India. It is also expected that India will become a major hub for the export of small cars throughout the world by 2020.

Turnover in the automotive industry is projected to grow rapidly, in terms of product range, export destinations and sources of imports. By 2020, it is anticipated that the industry would be worth $115 billion. Auto exports are expected to grow from $6.9 billion to $30 billion, and imports for the auto industry will be $35 billion. There are huge opportunities to put new plants in India; and those in the industry know what India is importing today in terms of high-technology products, on vehicle safety items, and fuel-injection systems. There is opportunity for the industry to start those plants, which would be localized, creating a new sector of business.

---

4. See slide 4 in Appendix A.

One of the megatrends in the automotive industry is in regulation, specifically on emissions, fuel-efficiency, safety, and recyclability. We may be about years years behind these laws, as compared to the laws in the United States, both on emissions and on safety. On fuel efficiency, the size of the vehicles in India is much smaller. The fuel efficiency concept is also very different in India as compared to the United States. Changing customer behavior and perceived quality are new concerns, as these were not issues in India until recently. All these issues will play a key role in the automotive industry going forward.

The Indian auto-component industry is expected to grow to $150 billion by 2020. Exports go more to Western Europe than elsewhere, and North America should touch around $9.5 billion. The auto-component industry contributes 2.9 percent of GDP, which will go to 3.6 percent. And the auto-component industry will create an additional 1.2 million jobs.

Several concepts still need innovation, specifically downsized engines and advanced transmissions. Any company has to innovate products for the Indian market; you cannot use the same large-size engines for India that are used in the United States. So you have to downsize it, but you still need to be far more fuel-efficient because that is what the Indian consumer demands.

Innovations are also happening in Indian component design. For example, the turbochargers, the air cooling systems, and the intake systems are all getting modified. A lot of innovation is going on in this sector.

Also, a new law will go into effect in India at the end of this fiscal year—March—on fuel efficiency. There will be benefits to the automobile companies if they achieve better fuel efficiency. So India will be ahead of many countries on the fuel-efficiency front, because that's a very, very key driver for the Indian economy.

A lot of U.S. companies want to come to India, because in the United States you have all the electronics for the vehicles, in the safety components, emission, air brakes, air conditioning. The electronic shift in the vehicle is increasingly higher. And that's a huge business—India has good electronic engineering manpower and skills. They are far more involved in the use of testing—endurance testing and safety testing. If American companies want to come to India, I think this is a good area to [consider].

Operational excellence is a key issue in India because today the productivity of Indian workers is far lower than the productivity of workers in China. I have plants both in India and in China, so I can tell you with my own experience. But there is a huge need for skills to be developed in this area on lean supply chains and manufacturing skills.

A lot of companies have worked on this; 21 companies in India have Deming Awards, which is the highest award for quality excellence. India is second only to Japan in Deming awards, which means some of the industries have learned this skill. But this has to be learned by many more companies and industries yet.

Automotive and industry associations are developing centers all over India in order for more potential employees to benefit from learning these skills. In the automotive industry, the challenges are that the margins are becoming lower because the price of the raw materials is going up. And the market is not able to afford additional price, so you have to come up with more innovative ideas on cost reduction.

One of the key challenges in the automotive industry today is the manpower churn. Because of the number of opportunities available, people are leaving from one company to the other at the management level, and at the workers level it is becoming a major issue. So, concerted HR activities are required in the industry today.

Larger companies have structured this, but medium and small-scale industries, which are key for India's growth, are where this is really lagging. A lot of partnerships are now being formed; the best partnerships done today in India are by Maruti Suzuki and by Tata Motors.

They are helping small-scale industry. Actually, they are posting their offices in the small-scale industries virtually on a full-time basis for a couple of years, helping them put systems in place on quality and manufacturing systems and hand-holding senior management so that they move up the supply chain. It also benefits the manufacturers because they get a consistent quality.

Up to 36 percent of available jobs remain vacant for want of candidates with the requisite skill. On the one hand, we say that we have X level of unemployment, but the overall industry still has a large number of people who need to be recruited. So headhunters or recruiters who match people with jobs have a huge business in India, but it is difficult to get good skill. So a lot of work is happening on this front, and I think the biggest challenge is to train and retain this talent.

I will give you a small example, and this is the first in the auto-component industry in India. This is in my own company [Tata AutoComp Systems]; we have developed a skill-development center, which is only about six months old, with the National Council of Training and Vocational Training with the government of India. And as per Tata Group policy, we give priority to people who are economically backward. This is also being monitored at the Tata Son's, Ltd. level [chairman's office of the Tata Group]: how much employment we are creating for the weakest section of society.

But just giving employment serves no purpose to us unless we train them. So we are running a skill-development center, and the government of India is funding most of the training.

So what do we do? We take people for three years' training. It's an earn-and-learn skill; so they work two months in class, then four months on the shop floor, then 15 days in class, again four months on the shop floor. So the training matches exactly the job they're doing, and they get a certification. At the end of it, he will have more than six months' classroom training and the practical training of the shop. The six-month training is actually paid by the government of India.

After we started this, a lot of other industries have now taken the initiative. Actually, how to do this itself was an issue. So the Tata Group has taken the lead in trying to educate a lot of industries that this is a good idea, to do it, and there is a good support from government in this respect.

And it is not only for us. We just give them a certificate after three years. We can keep them permanently if they want. But with that certificate, they can go to any company in the industry.

So the national manufacturing policy is [supposed] to increase the manufacturing portion of India's GDP to 25 percent by 2022, create 100 million additional jobs and increase the level of domestic value-addition and technology depth in manufacturing. And [part of] the technology depth in manufacturing is that you have to modify your technology for the Indian market.

The CEO of Daimler in India mentioned to me that they have a lot of issues with their trucks' quality, and so there are a lot of German guys coming in, looking at the issue of quality. So now in Stuttgart it is fine, but the Indians don't know how to do welding! So there is a welding issue. But [the] welding was not bad—I won't say it was 100 percent as good as what was done in Stuttgart, but it was nearly 90 percent-plus. And they realized that the application of the vehicle was much different. So the CEO was telling me that he sent people in the market, and they found out that the vehicle was being used in a much different way than it is designed for. And so those small innovations and these small modifications of new technology are required.

There are national investments in manufacturing zones that are being created, and this will become a special-purpose vehicle and I think this will really change the bandwidth of the manufacturing sector in India. So the integrated industrial townships of at least 5,000 hectares of land, state-of-the-art infrastructure, land-use based on zoning—because acquiring land is a major issue—and so the government is working on this. And at least 30 percent of the total land area will be for the manufacturing units in the industrial corridors.

The Delhi-Mumbai corridor you are well aware of. If you were not aware, I will just show you from here to Delhi to Mumbai, this whole corridor, which is shown in the light-brown color.[5] So huge activity, the whole industrial path is being created here in the corridor. Thirty percent of the land will be used for manufacturing industry. The government is making a structure, the private industry is participating in this structure, and the skill-development centers—Gujarat is leading in this today in the skill-development center—and the corridor is crossing through Rajasthan and Madhya Pradesh, which are not so developed states in India. And so huge activities are happening in those states as well.

Doing Business in India

I would say India will change geometrically, not arithmetically. It's just a matter of plus or minus one or two years in a 10-to-15-year horizon. And so it is a Tata Group policy that we need to invest ahead of the curve. So sizing the future by leapfrogging is what I would like to say.

And as you see in China, over the last 10 years the growth in China has been extremely high as soon as they crossed the per-capita income of $2,400; that's a threshold for major growth. In India the per capita is at $1,500. As soon as we touch that per-capita income, you can see the growth will be really in a geometrical progression.

What got you here will not get you there: look at leapfrogging opportunities. Technology adaption is more important than quick returns. The Dreamliner is a revolutionary product that had its share of struggles. Three, four years it was behind schedule, but it is an outstanding product.

Doing and learning is more important than knowledge acquisition. Mr. Tata had a dream, actually, of this car to be made in plastics [referring to the Tata Nano]. And some things were made with plastics, but it was not fully successful—not from a safety point of view. But from a cost point of view, we found that steel doors and a steel body was cheaper. Not that we have dropped this project of a plastic body; we are still working on it. And that's why I say to you that you have to really innovate [for] the Indian market.

Imagining the future is more important than forecasting it, and uncertainty is in the normal state of nature. I would believe that—efficiency versus effectiveness—you should work on things you don't quite understand. You find it difficult to plan, as the way forward is unclear.

And so I would say that if you look at a fly, a fly cannot fly in a straight line—only human beings look at the straight line. If you look at most of the animals, birds and insects, they look in

5. See slide 5 in Appendix A.

APPENDIX B
SPEAKER BIOGRAPHICAL INFORMATION

Vikram Singh Mehta
Chairman, Shell Group of Companies, India

Vikram Mehta's career began in the Indian Administrative Service (IAS), government of India, in 1978. He resigned that position in 1980 and joined Philips Petroleum in the UK. In 1984 he returned to India to join the state-owned Oil India as adviser for strategic planning. Mehta joined Shell International in London in 1988 and was posted as the managing director for Shell markets and chemicals in Egypt from 1991 to 1993. In 1994, he became the chairman of the Shell Group of Companies in India.

Mehta is a member of the National Council of the Confederation of Indian Industry (CII) and serves as chairman of its hydrocarbons committee. He is on the boards of Colgate Palmolive India Limited, the Indian Public Schools' Society, the Pandit Deendayal University of Petroleum, and the Fletcher School of Law & Diplomacy at Tufts University. Mehta was also a recipient of Asia House's "Businessman of the Year 2010" award.

Rajiv Lall
Managing Director & CEO, Infrastructure Development Finance Company Ltd.

Rajiv Lall is the managing director and chief executive officer of IDFC. He has held this position since January 2005. Lall has more than two decades of experience with leading global investment banks, multilateral agencies, and academia. His areas of expertise include project finance, private equity/venture capital, international capital markets, trade, infrastructure, and macroeconomic policy issues, with a focus on emerging markets including India and China in particular.

Lall chairs the Infrastructure Council of CII (Confederation of Indian Industry), a leading business chamber in the country, and was president of the Bombay Chamber of Commerce and Industry. Lall is India's representative to the G20 Workgroup on Infrastructure and a member of the City of London's Advisory Council for India. He is also member of the Planning Commission's Steering Committee on Urban Development Management set up to help formulate the country's 12th Five-Year Plan; the prime minister's Committees on Infrastructure Finance and Transport Sector Development; and the Reserve Bank of India's Committee on Non-Banking Financial Companies.

John Flannery
President & CEO, GE India

John Flannery is the president and CEO for General Electric India and is directly responsible for all of GE's operations in the country. Flannery has been with GE for more than 22 years and has held several senior leadership positions in the company. He has extensive experience in building and leading large teams and growing businesses in global assignments.

Prior to assuming his current role, Flannery was president and CEO of GE Capital Asia Pacific since January 2009. Before that, he was president and CEO of GE Commercial Finance, Asia. Previously, Flannery was managing director and business leader of the Bank Loan Group (BLG) for GE Corporate Financial Services, where he managed one of the largest global banks and institutional loan portfolios valued at nearly $10 billion.

Prior to joining BLG, Flannery was president and CEO of GE Equity, the private-equity arm of GE Capital, and before that held leadership positions in the leveraged finance and private-equity sectors, including two years as president and CEO, GE Capital Argentina and Chile.

Prathap C. Reddy
Chairman, Apollo Hospitals Group

Reddy founded Apollo Hospitals in Chennai in 1983 at a time when private health care institutions were virtually unknown in India. He has undertaken pioneering work in bringing about institutional changes in the private health care infrastructure by establishing Apollo Institutes for postgraduate medical and nursing education, hospital administration, physiotherapy, clinical research, and a large number of paramedical programs. With the setting up of the Apollo Telemedicine Networking Foundation, Health Super Hiway, Apollo Munich Insurance Co., and the Apollo Reach Hospitals, he helped establish a modern health care network through both in-house and outreach services, reaching out to millions of people.

Reddy has served on several CII (Confederation of Indian Industry) committees and councils, including as chairman of the National Healthcare Committee since 2006, chairman of the Health Council since 2010, and chairman of the National Council on Public Health since 2011 through which he provided the government with budget recommendations and supplemented government efforts in the area of public health and in developing health insurance systems.

Reddy has received a number of esteemed awards and recognitions, including the Padma Bhushan from the government of India in 1991 for his contribution to the emergence of the private health care system, and the prestigious Padma Vibhushan in March 2010, the second-highest civilan award given by the government of India.

Arvind Goel

President & Head, Business Group, Tata Autocomp Systems Ltd.

Goel is the president and head, Business Group of Tata AutoComp (Automotive Components) Systems Ltd. He has previously held a number of positions within Tata AutoComp, including as chairman of TACO Hendrickson Suspensions Ltd, chairman of Nanjing TACO, board member for Taco Industrial Services Ltd, and director of Tata Toyo Radiators Ltd. Prior to joining Tata, Goel served as the president and chief operating officer of MAN Force Trucks.

Goel received his bachelor's degree in mechanical engineering from the National Institute of Technology–Krukshetra, and has graduated from leadership and management programs at Tata Management and Training Center conducted in conjunction with the Stern School of Business at NYU and the Harvard Business School. He is an active participant in the Society of Indian Automobile Manufacturers (SIAM), and next year will serve on the National Executive Committee for the Association of Automotive Component Manufacturers (ACMA).

www.ingramcontent.com/pod-product-compliance
Ingram Content Group UK Ltd.
Pitfield, Milton Keynes, MK11 3LW, UK
UKHW051418150926
475561UK00005B/231